DRAWING MADE FUN

REPTILES

Robin Lee Makowski

Rourke

Publishing LLC

Vero Beach, Florida 32964

www.rourkepublishing.com

All illustrations Robin Lee Makowski.

Editor: Frank Sloan

Cover design by Nicola Stratford

Library of Congress Cataloging-in-Publication Data

Makowski, Robin Lee.
 Reptiles / written and illustrated by Robin Lee Makowski.
   p. cm. -- (Drawing made fun)
 ISBN 1-59515-473-6 (hardcover)
 1. Reptiles in art--Juvenile literature. 2. Drawing--Technique--Juvenile literature. I. Title.
  NC783.8.R54M349 2006
  743.6'79--dc22

                              2005010725

Printed in the USA

CG/CG

Rourke Publishing
1-800-394-7055
www.rourkepublishing.com
sales@rourkepublishing.com
Post Office Box 3328, Vero Beach, FL 32964

INTRODUCTION

Drawing is a skill that is fun and useful, and something everyone wants to learn how to do better.

The step-by-step instructions in this book will help you first to see what you want to draw. Then you can place the parts correctly so your finished drawing looks the way you want it to. Of course, the only way to perfect your drawing skills is to practice, practice, practice!

If the drawing doesn't look right the first time, draw it again. It can be frustrating if the finished drawing doesn't look the way you wanted it to and you don't know how to fix it.

Follow the instructions and have fun learning how to draw your favorite reptiles!

MATERIALS

The two most common problems with drawing are not seeing how the parts of the object line up and using the wrong materials. The first problem will be solved with practice. The second problem is much easier to fix. You'll have a lot more fun and success with your drawings if you're not fighting with hard pencils, dry erasers, and thin paper.

These materials are available almost anywhere and will make your practice much easier:

Best to Use
Soft Pencils (#2B or softer)
Thick and Thin Drawing Pens
Soft White Eraser or Kneaded Eraser
Pencil Sharpener
Drawing Paper Tablet
Tracing Paper
Wax-Free Graphite Paper (helpful but not necessary)
Crayons or Colored Pencils or Colored Markers

More Difficult to Use
Typing or Computer Paper
Hard or Pink Erasers
Hard Pencils (if the pencil will mark your hand, it's soft enough)

HOW TO START

The Shapes of Things

Everything you draw in this book will start with larger geometric shapes to get the proportions and to get everything lined up correctly. Then the details will emerge from there. One of the biggest mistakes made when drawing is starting with the outline. By the time the outline is finished, the proportions are way off.

You'll use both standard geometric shapes and free-form shapes to start:

Laying Down the Lines

You can do your preliminary drawing—and make your mistakes—on tracing paper and then transfer it to the drawing paper. If you draw directly on the drawing paper, you can keep your drawing clean by putting a piece of scrap paper under your hand so you don't smear the pencil as you work.

When you start your drawing, use light lines so you can erase. Your preliminary shapes do not need to be perfect—they are only guidelines for your final drawing. Make sure everything lines up!

Tracing paper will take a lot of erasing. To transfer your preliminary drawing, use wax-free graphite paper between the tracing paper and drawing paper. Be sure the graphite side is down!

Draw back over the lines with a colored pencil so you don't miss transferring part of it. If you don't have graphite paper, turn over your drawing and draw with your soft pencil back over the lines. Turn it right side up; place it on the drawing paper and trace back over the lines with a colored pencil. You will have a nice, clean drawing to finish.

FINISHING

To make things easier to see and follow in the book, you can use drawing pens for the final step. Below are examples of strokes you can use if you want to finish your drawing and some tricks for making your drawings look dimensional. You can stop at Step 3 of each lesson and color your drawing, if you wish, by following the color instructions for each reptile. You can use crayons, colored pencils, or markers. If you use markers, color the drawing first. Then finish by drawing the lines over the color with your drawing pen. You will love the results!

> You will be learning how to draw reptiles in this book. Have fun!

Practice laying down tone with your art pen by tracing around a popsicle stick to make a tone chart. 0% is white paper and 100% is solid black. For crosshatching, use thin, parallel lines that overlap as the tone gets darker:

For stippling, use the very tip of the pen to make tiny dots. Don't bang the pen hard on the paper; use a light touch to keep the dots round. Use fewer dots farther apart for lighter areas and heavier dots closer together for dark areas.
Warning: Stippling takes a long time but is worth the effort!

Now try to make the same shape look dimensional with your strokes:

Alligator

"Gators" are very large reptiles living in the Southeastern United States. Their cousins, the crocodiles, are more numerous and widespread. Alligators usually grow to 12 feet (3.6 meters), but much larger animals have been reported. They can live in fresh, brackish (mix of salt and fresh) water or saltwater ponds and estuaries. Gators hunt fish, but will feed on small mammals and birds, if available.

1. Begin with a long oval for the head, connected to a potato shape for the body. Add the shapes for the legs, feet, and tail, as shown.

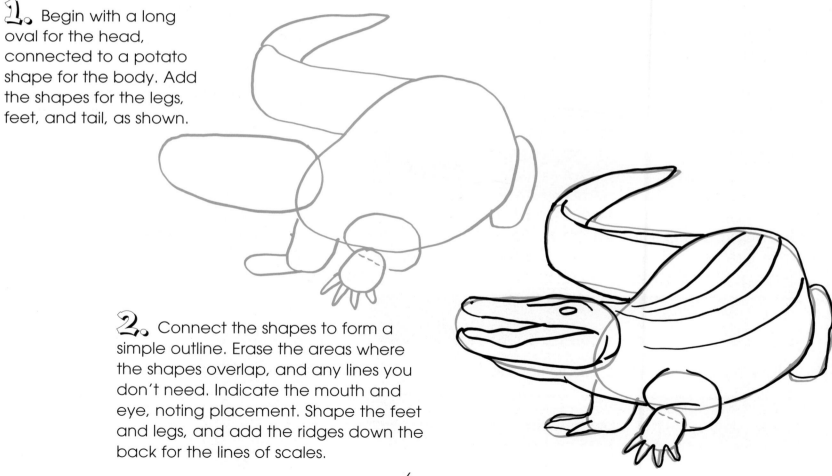

2. Connect the shapes to form a simple outline. Erase the areas where the shapes overlap, and any lines you don't need. Indicate the mouth and eye, noting placement. Shape the feet and legs, and add the ridges down the back for the lines of scales.

6

3. Draw in the teeth and scales on the back ridges. Draw in the rows on the sides and belly as a guide where to draw the scales. Use a criss-cross pattern on the legs to indicate scales. Small, connected circles make great scales. Use a sharp pencil or fine-tipped pen for this step. If you want to color your Alligator, finish the scales and add your colors, or color then add the scales on top.

Tip: For scale detail, make sure you contour, or curve, rows of scales around the shapes of the reptiles. Straight lines will make the reptiles look flat; contoured lines will give your drawing volume and make it look dimensional.

4. Use short strokes to indicate tone on the scales, paying attention to the fact that there are light and dark patterns within the scale detail.

For Color: Alligator hatchlings (babies) are green and yellow striped, while adults are dark gray with dirty yellowish belly scales. The older the gator gets, the less the pattern is apparent.

Chameleon

Chameleons are members of a varied family of tree-dwelling reptiles. All chameleons are insect-eaters, moving slowly through the trees and nabbing their prey with a tongue that's longer than their body! Chameleons, like some other lizards, have the ability to change color with temperature and surroundings for perfect camouflage.

1. Start with a rounded triangle shape for the body. Add a circle for the prehensile tail and an egg shape for the head. Notice how some of the feet shapes are coming under the branch. Indicate the eye and notice the placement.

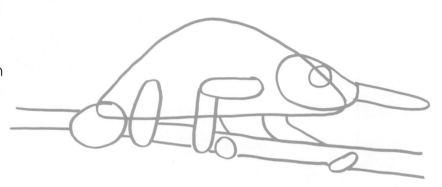

2. Connect the shapes to form a simple outline. Erase the areas where the shapes overlap, and any lines you don't need. Draw in the rest of the legs and feet, as shown. Indicate the eyes and the mouth. Shape the horns. Curl the tail around the branch.

3. Detail the eyes and head. Indicate the scales and tonal pattern. Shape the branch. If you want to color your Chameleon, stop drawing at this point and switch to your colors, then draw the scale detail over the top.

For Color:
Chameleons are mainly green, but can have a variety of colors from yellow to aqua to pink to purple.

4. To finish the drawing, use stippling to draw in the tone. Leave the outer scales white. Add the striations (light and dark lines) to the horns. Detail the concentric circles around the eye.

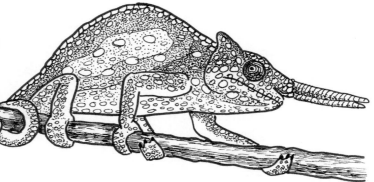

9

Diamondback Rattlesnake

We will be creating a portrait of this Diamondback, the largest of the rattlesnakes. A segment of the rattle is created each time the snake sheds. At one time it was believed that the snake's age could be told by counting the segments on the rattle, but this is not true. While the Rattler's bite can kill in defense, the snake would prefer to save its venom for hunting its prey. When approached, the snake will shake the rattle to create a buzzing sound to ward off enemies.

1. Establish the box shape to contain the portrait. Begin with a long, tapering shape that's blunt on the right for the head. Extend the rattle outside the box for an interesting composition and add the rest of the preliminary lines. Pay special attention to placement and sizes!

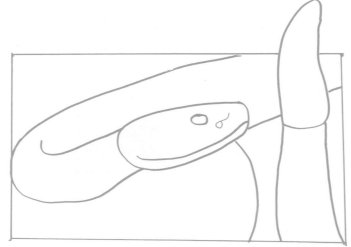

2. Connect the shapes to form a simple outline. Erase the areas where the shapes overlap, and any lines you don't need. Indicate the eye and line of the mouth, paying special attention to placement. Connect the shapes and define the segmented tail. Indicate the pattern. Start the scale detail on the face and around the mouth, including the heat pit near the nose.

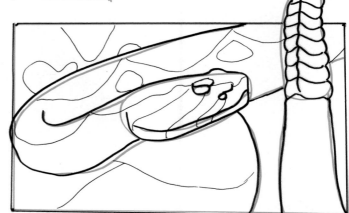

3. This is where it can get tricky! Draw in light, parallel lines indicating the scale growth. These lines are meant as a guide for lining up the scales. Begin to draw in the scale pattern on the face. Use a criss-cross pattern to indicate the tiny scales on the tail in front of the rattle. Add the forked tongue. If you want to color your Diamondback, stop drawing at this point and switch to your colors.

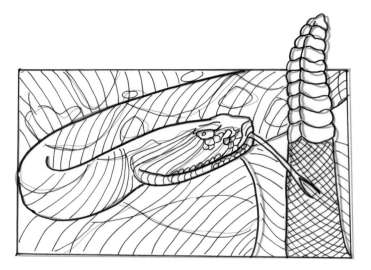

Remember: Lining up all your shapes in the right spot will result in work you will be very happy with! Take the extra few minutes in the first steps to make sure everything is in the right place. Draw, erase, and draw again!

For Color: Diamondbacks are gray with black, tan, yellowish, and white markings.

4. To finish the drawing, use long ovals to indicate the scales. Rattlers have "keeled" scales, or a little ridge down the middle of each scale. Leave the lighter scales light. If you get too much tone, you'll end up with a blob. Use short strokes for the detail on the rattle.

Gaboon Viper

Native to Africa, Gaboon Vipers are heavy-bodied snakes. Although it's a large snake, it's short in relation to its girth. The Gaboon Viper has a beautiful pattern that blends perfectly with the leaf litter where the snake lives. Camouflaged so perfectly, it waits for prey that it will strike at with long, 2-inch (5-centimeter) fangs, which are the longest fangs of any snake!

1. Begin with a large oval for the body and a smaller oval inset for the head. Since the snake curves back on itself, use lines to indicate the curves, as shown. Place the eye.

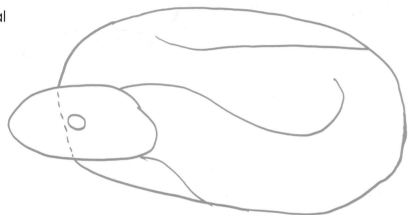

2. Connect the shapes to form a simple outline. Erase the areas where the shapes overlap, and any lines you don't need. Shape the mouth and add the horn-shaped scales near the nose. There will not be much scale detail with this drawing; however, the pattern will take some work. Draw in simple shapes: a stripe down the back, stripes at intervals down the sides, the shield shapes down the white back stripe with the X shapes, and the mask from the eye to the mouth. Add the pupil slit in the eye.

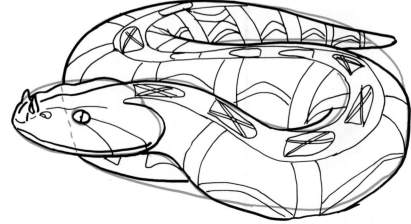

12

3. Erase the overlapping lines where the patterns intersect; in other words, most of the white areas will touch each other. Indicate the scales around the top of the mouth. If you want to color your Gaboon Viper, stop drawing at this point and switch to your colors.

Author's Note: Do you get confused when it comes time to add the color? Do you end up coloring the wrong shape? Me too! I like to put a little light X in the shapes where I'll end up adding color or tone. It really helps!

For Color: Gaboon Vipers are white with black, tan, and yellowish markings.

4. This snake will be better in color, but to finish the drawing, use short strokes to indicate tone. Use the same stroke in the dark areas as in the light ones; just use more strokes closer together. Use stippling on the belly and head to indicate shading.

13

Giant Tortoise

Giant Tortoises are only found in two remote places on earth. These giant herbivores slowly roam large territories, grazing and looking for water. With no natural enemies, they can live for 200 years!

1. Begin with a rock shape that's flat on the bottom. The head is a small circle. Use ovals for the legs and a small circle for the eye.

Tip: If it doesn't look right when you start, keep going! Think about the difference in a cake before and after it's baked. A drawing just started is like cake batter: keep working on it and you'll like it a lot better when it's done. And if it's not exactly the way you want it, spend the time and try again!

2. Connect the shapes to form a simple outline. Erase the areas where the shapes overlap, and any lines you don't need. Indicate the front of the plastron (bottom part of the shell) and the wrinkles in the neck. Add the mouth line. Draw in the massive legs, toenails, and indicate the scales on the shell.

3. Detail the scales on the head, wrinkles on the neck, and scales on the legs, using various sized circles that touch one another. Notice how the largest scales are on the front of the legs; it helps to draw these in first! If you want to color your Giant Tortoise, stop drawing at this point and switch to your colors.

For Color: Giant Tortoises have a gray shell on the back, and tough gray-green scales on the rest of the body. You can use some yellowish color on the highlights on the shell scales, and put your Tortoise in a field of flowers for color.

4. To finish the drawing, use short strokes across each larger scale on the legs and head. Use a pattern of strokes on each scale on the shell. Notice how the tone is NOT taken to the edge of each scale. If you do that, you'll lose your details.

15

Gila Monster

Gila (pronounced HEE luh) Monsters and their cousins, the Beaded Lizards, are the only two venomous lizards. With a beaded pattern that warns predators, Gila Monsters venture boldly into bird and rodent nests, eating everything from the eggs to the adults. With no fangs, Gilas have to chew the venom into their prey, and once they bite down, they don't let go!

1. Begin with a flat oval for the main body shape. Use a circle for the head, the tail shape, and the ovals for the legs.

2. Connect the shapes to form a simple outline. Erase the areas where the shapes overlap, and any lines you don't need. Shape the head, and add the eye and mouth. Shape the legs and add the feet and toes. Shape the tail.

3. Refine the outline and indicate the coloration. Add scale detail to the head, noticing that the largest scales are around the mouth and on the front of the head. If you want to color your Gila Monster, stop drawing at this point and switch to your colors.

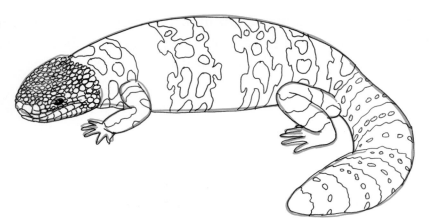

For Color: Gilas are black and bright yellow.

4. Yikes! This looks like a lot of work! It takes a while, but the steps are simple. For the yellow parts, just use little circles and make sure to line them up around the Gila. For the black parts, make your little circles and go round and round the circle to fill it in, leaving a highlight. On the large head scales, leave the top margins: don't color all the way to all the edges of the scale or you'll lose detail.

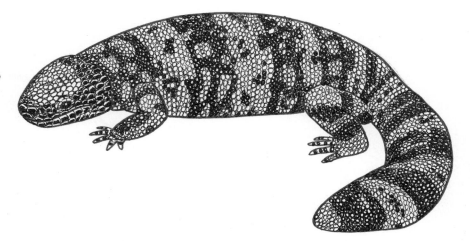

Gopher Tortoise

As the name implies, this tortoise will dig a giant burrow for itself where it rests and retains body heat at night when it's cooler. Gopher Tortoises often share their burrows with other reptiles such as rattlesnakes. During the day, they feed on plants and hide from predators by pulling themselves completely into their shells.

1. Begin with a large oval for the body, and smaller ovals for the head and front leg.

2. Connect the shapes to form a simple outline. Erase the areas where the shapes overlap, and any lines you don't need. Add the mouth and place the eye. Shape the shell and front leg.

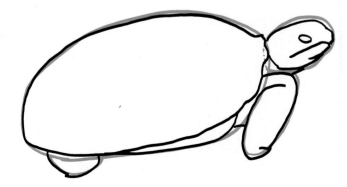

18

3. Add the scale details on the legs and scale pattern on the shell. Start to detail the shell, as shown. If you want to color your Gopher Tortoise, stop drawing at this point and switch to your colors.

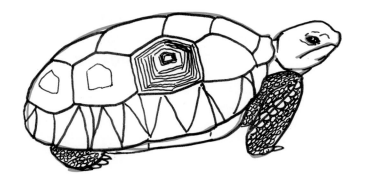

For Color: Gopher Tortoises are tan to gray on the shell with gray scales on the head and legs.

4. To finish the drawing, use short strokes on the head for tone, paying attention to the light. Add tone to the leg scales, but keep that margin between them or you'll lose detail.

Green Anole

There are many species of Anoles (pronounced ANN olz) living in the Southeastern United States, but the Green Anole is the only native. Anoles are small lizards that hunt insects. Sometimes gardeners will find a cluster of tiny, long eggs in their flowerpots. Anoles, like most reptiles, lay their eggs and leave. When the hatchlings emerge, they're on their own.

1. Begin with a large, elongated oval for the body with a cone shape for the head. Use free forms for the tail and legs. Add the shape for the "sail," or dewlap, under the chin.

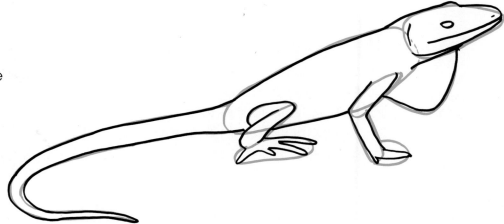

2. Connect the shapes to form a simple outline. Erase the areas where the shapes overlap, and any lines you don't need. Shape the face and add the eye and mouth. Shape the legs and feet.

3. Draw in lines indicating coloration and detail the face. Refine the drawing. If you want to color your Green Anole, stop drawing at this point and switch to your colors.

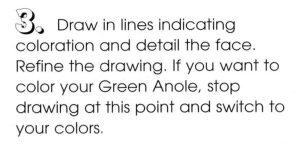

For Color: Green Anoles are lime to Kelly green above and yellow to cream below. The dewlap below the chin is bright red outlined in yellow.

Tip: The tinier the dots you use to stipple, the better your drawing will look. Don't lose patience! It takes some time, but it's worth it.

4. To finish the drawing, stipple in the coloration, paying attention to the treatment of tone on the belly.

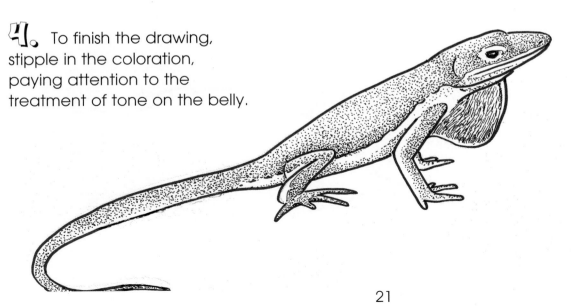

Horned Lizard

Horned Lizards are native to the American Southwest. These tough little lizards have adapted to their desert environment. Their coloration blends in perfectly with their environment. They can run very fast, and even when something catches up with them, the sharp little spikes covering their bodies deliver a painful sting to predators.

1. Begin with a large, thick oval for the body. Use a small circle for the head and free forms for the legs and tail.

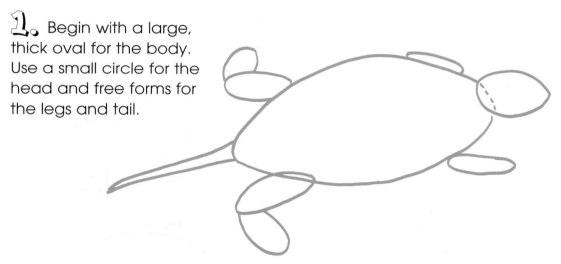

2. Connect the shapes to form a simple outline. Erase the areas where the shapes overlap, and any lines you don't need. Draw in the sharp spines at the back of the head and detail the feet. Add the eye.

3. Indicate the pattern on the back and legs. If you want to color your Horned Lizard, stop drawing and switch to your colors.

4. To finish the drawing, use short strokes or stippling to indicate pattern. Add the spines near the tail.

Iguana

There are several species of Iguanas, one of the most popular reptiles kept as a pet. Green Iguanas are omnivorous, which means they'll eat anything, but the main part of their diet is green leaves and flowers. An Iguana uses its long, spiked tail as a whip against enemies. If a predator grabs onto the tail, Iguanas, like some other lizards, will shake the tail off and grow a new one, except for the bones, which cannot regenerate. We will create a portrait of the author's own Iguana, Mojo.

1. Start with an egg shape for the head and place the eye and mouth. Use lines to indicate the other shapes.

2. Connect the shapes to form two simple outlines. Erase the areas where the shapes overlap, and any lines you don't need. Detail the eye and shape the mouth, paying attention to placement. Add the facial scales and indicate the spikes on the back.

24

3. Shape the eye. Indicate where tone will change on the body with light lines. Add the spikes on the dewlap and back. If you want to color Mojo, stop drawing at this point and switch to your colors.

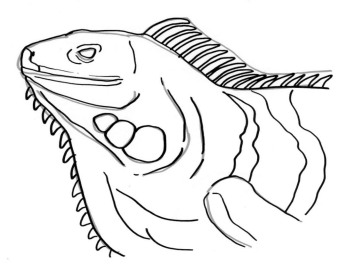

Tip: If you're having trouble figuring out what's wrong with your drawing, walk away from it and come back to it, or hold it up to a mirror. The mistakes will jump out at you!

For Color: Green Iguanas can change color, depending on the temperature and if they're in direct sunlight. The green ranges from emerald to olive to fluorescent! They have black, sometimes orange, and sometimes tan markings.

4. Detail the scales. This will take some time, but it's not as bad as it looks! Use lines to indicate the tone on the back where the scales are very tiny, almost like sandpaper.

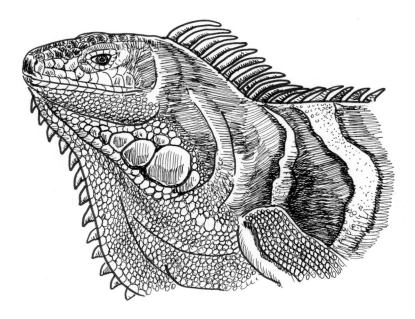

Komodo Dragon

Komodo Dragons are the largest of all living lizards. Living on very isolated islands, Komodo Dragons are a protected species. Visitors to the Island of Komodo are warned to heed these large, fast monitors! They have been known to attack and kill humans.

1. Begin with a large circle for the body and an oval for the head. Connect the shapes with the lines for the neck.

2. Connect the shapes to form a simple outline. Erase the areas where the shapes overlap, and any lines you don't need. Add the mouth and the eyes. Add the long legs and toes. Use a triangle shape for the tail.

26

3. Detail the drawing and sharpen the large toenails. Add the tiny spikes on the tail. If you want to color your Komodo Dragon, stop drawing and switch to your colors.

For Color: Komodo Dragons are greenish gray.

4. To finish the drawing, use short strokes or stippling to indicate tone. Scales on this large monitor are very small.

King Cobra

The King Cobra is native to India and is the largest of all venomous snakes, growing to a possible length of 18 feet (5.5 meters)! This snake can rear up to a third of its length to ward off even the tallest enemy. Its diet consists of other snakes and rodents. Baby cobras are born with enough venom to kill.

1. Begin with an oval shape for the hood and a long oval for the head. Add the "S" shape for the body, as shown.

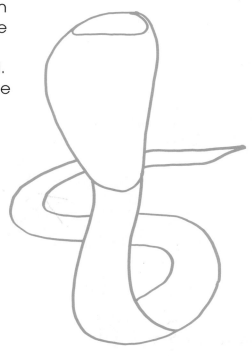

2. Connect the shapes to form a simple outline. Erase the areas where the shapes overlap, and any lines you don't need. Add the eye and indicate the spread hood.

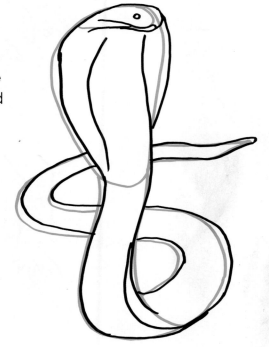

3. Add the belly scales and scale detail on the face. Add the eye spots on the hood. If you want to color your King Cobra, stop drawing and switch to your colors.

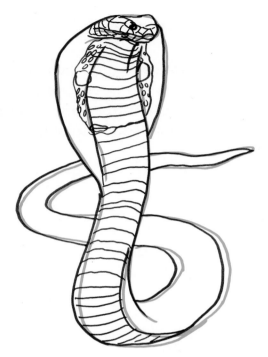

For Color: King Cobras are warm gray with cream and yellow belly scales, and brown and tan across the back of the hood with black details. Some banding on the body may be apparent.

Remember: Lining up all your shapes in the right spot will result in work you will be very happy with! Take the extra few minutes in the first steps to make sure everything is in the right place. Draw, erase, and draw again!

4. To finish the drawing, you can use short lines to indicate the tone, following the contours of the snake. Use heavier strokes for the darker areas and lighter, thinner strokes for the medium tones. Use a light criss-cross pattern to indicate scales on the snake's back.

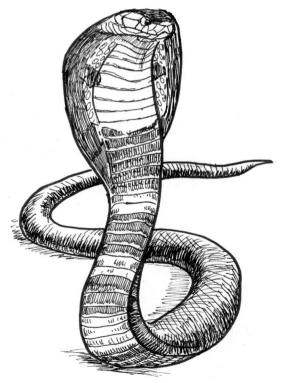

Leatherback Sea Turtle

Leatherbacks are the largest member of the turtle and tortoise family. These giants can grow to a length of 8 or more feet (2.4 meters)! They spend their entire life in the ocean, and only the females return to the beach where they were hatched to lay their eggs. Leatherbacks are covered with barnacles and feed on jellyfish and other stinging sea creatures.

1. Begin with an upside-down teardrop shape for the shell. Add the free-form shapes for the head and flippers.

2. Connect the shapes to form a simple outline. Erase the areas where the shapes overlap, and any lines you don't need. Shape the head, flippers, and shell. Add the eye.

3. Further refine the outline. Add the five ridges down the back and the barnacles on the flippers. If you want to color your Leatherback Sea Turtle, stop drawing and switch to your colors.

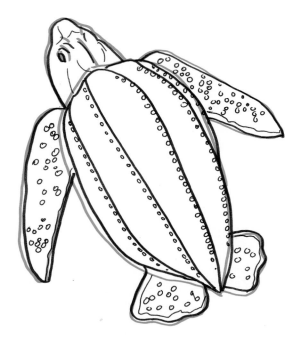

For Color:
Leatherback Sea Turtles have dark gray shells and gray skin with white markings for the barnacles.

4. To finish the drawing, use short strokes or stippling for tone. Leave the outside margins of the flippers light, as well as the top of the head.

ABOUT THE ARTIST

Robin Lee Makowski is a professional artist, illustrator, and instructor. She specializes in watercolor painting and drawing and has illustrated more than thirty children's books.

"I always loved science and nature," explains the artist. "I studied everything closely and tried to draw it. I noticed the way things lined up, how close or far away things were, the way the light hit them, and how the light affected the color."

"It's so important to learn how to draw," she insists. "You have to realize that when you can draw, you're free. All you need is a pencil and paper and you can create wherever you are. Drawing is rewarding both in the process and the product."

Robin lives in Hobe Sound, Florida, with her hus-band, two sons, and her best friend, her mutt Casey.

Visit Robin at her website: www.rlmart.com